Who's at the screen of the crime?
Get the answer in
**MODEM MENACE**

A trip into the wilderness can get pretty wild!
See why in
**TERROR TRAIL**

Here's a job that will really haunt you.
Check out
**GRAVE DISCOVERY**

Who's *really* behind the wall?
See for yourself in
**A BONE TO PICK**

Who's calling? Get the answer, read
**PLEASE CALL BACK!**

Somebody's inside . . . but nobody should be.
See who in
**ANYBODY HOME?**

Someone's planning an *un*welcome.
Find out more in
**HOME, CREEPY, HOME**

Shop . . . until you drop! Read all about it in
**BUYING TROUBLE**

ISBN 0-8114-9304-0
Copyright ©1995 Steck-Vaughn Company. All rights reserved. No part of the material protected by this copyright may be reproduced or utilized in any form or by any means, electronic or mechanical, including photocopying, recording, or by any information storage and retrieval system, without permission in writing from the copyright owner. Requests for permission to make copies of any part of the work should be mailed to: Copyright Permissions, Steck-Vaughn Company, P.O. Box 26015, Austin, TX 78755. Printed in the United States of America.

4 5 6 7 8 9 98

Produced by Mega-Books of New York, Inc.
Design and Art Direction by Michaelis/Carpelis Design Assoc.

Cover illustration: Wayne Alfano

# SEE NO EVIL

by Leslie McGuire

interior illustrations by
Cornelius Van Wright

# **CHAPTER 1**

"Wow!" thought Max. "Sebastian is playing Mozart's Concerto Number 24 in E Minor."

Max Burnett stood up from his piano and crossed the room. Then he put his ear to the wall so he could hear the music better. The wall tingled with the notes. Max sighed because the music sounded so perfect.

Music was Max's life. He loved classical music. Max and his mother were lucky to live in the L-shaped apartment next to Sebastian Wales. Sebastian was a competition pianist.

Sebastian was getting ready for a competition this weekend. The music

Max was listening to through the wall changed easily from Mozart to Bach. Max listened closely. He had learned most of what he knew by listening to Sebastian practice. Max heard the timing change in the complex Bach piece.

Max really liked that musical change. It made the music sound much sadder. It was as if a lonely voice was calling out from the apartment next door.

All of a sudden the doorbell rang.

"Who's *that*," Max groaned. He really didn't want to miss any of Sebastian's music.

"Who's there?" he called out.

"It's me, Dave," came a voice. "Hey, dude, open up!"

Max groaned again. Dave was the kid who lived upstairs. Dave was always hanging around and bothering Max. And he was always asking Max what it was like to be blind. Did Max see colors? Did he even know what colors were? Did he know the shapes of different things?

Sometimes Max wished Dave would just leave him alone. Too bad Dave couldn't figure that out. Now here he was again. Max opened the door slowly.

"Hey, I just got a whole new slab of really great clay," Dave said. He didn't even wait for Max to invite him in. He just walked right past Max and flopped down on the couch. "We could start your art lessons today!"

Max didn't want to start art lessons today, or any day. Dave thought he was an artist. He thought he could teach Max the shapes of things using clay. Max didn't care about the shapes of things. All he cared about was music.

"I can't today," said Max. He was still holding the door open. "I have to practice."

"Oh, come on," said Dave angrily. "All you ever want to do is play the piano day and night! You should try something else."

"And all you ever want to do is work with clay day and night," snapped Max. "I'm a musician, so I have to do what I have to do!"

Max sighed with relief when Dave charged out of the apartment. He slammed the door behind Dave and eased his way back to the piano.

Max sat down and got ready to play. He wanted to work out the Bach piece Sebastian was now playing. Max

wanted to play the piece just the way Sebastian was playing it. Sebastian's timing was really great.

At least it started out great. But then Sebastian started dragging the notes.

"How weird," thought Max. He couldn't figure out how Sebastian got his piano to drag the notes like that. He listened more carefully. The notes kept dragging.

"It must be some new fingering," Max decided. Just then Sebastian went back to playing the notes in the Bach piece perfectly.

Max smiled. "I guess he didn't like the new fingering much," he said to himself. "I didn't like it that much either."

# **CHAPTER 2**

Max woke up late the next morning. At first he thought the television was on. He could hear loud voices. The voices seemed angry. Then he heard thumps. It sure didn't sound like Saturday morning TV programs to him.

Max sat up in bed and listened. The voices were definitely not on the TV. He scrambled out of bed. As Max worked his way through the living room, he could hear the murmur of voices in the hall. He heard his mother's voice.

"What's going on?" Max wondered. He moved more quickly toward the voices and the door.

"This is insane! Get your hands off

me!" he heard a man shout.

Max's eyes widened in surprise. It was Sebastian Wales!

"I tell you, I didn't do it!" Sebastian was shouting more loudly now.

Max could hear Sebastian's cat, Ebony, meowing. "The poor animal

must be afraid," he thought.

Then another voice said, "You have the right to remain silent . . ."

"That's the police!" thought Max. "They're reading Sebastian his rights. He's being arrested!"

"Hey, dude, isn't this something?" Max turned toward Dave's voice.

All the neighbors were talking in the hall. "What's happening?" Max asked Dave.

Before Dave could answer, Max heard Sebastian screaming at someone.

"You'll hear from my lawyer! I'll have you charged with false arrest! Take your hands off of me!" screamed Sebastian as the police walked him out of the building.

This was terrible! Max couldn't imagine that his hero had done anything wrong. "Dave, what did Sebastian do?" asked Max.

"The police say he set fire to this guy Dirk Walton's house yesterday afternoon," Dave told Max. "The house burned to the ground and Walton's hands were really badly hurt."

"His hands? How awful!" said Max. "Dirk Walton is a famous competition pianist, just like Sebastian."

"Yeah," said Dave. "They say the Walton guy may never play the piano again. And they think Sebastian did it so Walton wouldn't be able to play in the competition this weekend."

"Sebastian would never do such a thing!" cried Max.

"Are you kidding, man?" said Dave. "That guy is intense."

"He is not!" shouted Max angrily. "He's a great pianist!"

"So what's that got to do with it?" asked Dave.

"This is crazy," yelled Max, defending his hero. "Sebastian isn't a criminal. A criminal could never play such great music!"

Max thought of all the times he'd

listened to Sebastian play. Then suddenly he remembered: Sebastian had been practicing for the competition yesterday afternoon! Max even remembered the music he was playing. First it was a piece by Mozart. Then it was a piece by Bach. Max turned on his heel and went into the apartment to find his mother.

Mrs. Burnett immediately called the police. Within half an hour, a detective was asking Max a million questions.

"Well, I guess that's it," said the detective after the questioning. "Your testimony will put Mr. Wales in the clear, Max."

"That's great! But I wonder who did do it then?" asked Max.

"I don't know yet," answered the detective. "But I do know that Mr. Wales is very lucky to have a fan like you."

Max could hardly wait for Sebastian Wales to come home.

# **CHAPTER**
# 3

On the morning news there was a short report about Dirk Walton's house burning down. The reporter said the police had a suspect in custody. The suspect said he was innocent. Then the news went on to baseball scores.

Max could hear Sebastian banging around inside his apartment. "He could have come over to thank me," thought Max, feeling a little put out. "Well, maybe he's too busy. Maybe he'll come by later," Max told himself.

Max started flipping through the TV channels. He was trying to find a science program to listen to.

All of a sudden the doorbell rang. Max

quickly turned off the TV and went to answer the door.

"Maybe this is Sebastian," Max thought excitedly. Sebastian would thank him for telling the police he was innocent. Then Max would get the chance to tell Sebastian how he really loved his playing and how much he learned from listening to him. They could finally have a real musician's talk.

As Max opened the door he had visions of what great friends he and Sebastian would become.

"Hey, dude," came Dave's voice. "What's happening?"

Max was disappointed it wasn't Sebastian. Well, at least he could tell Dave how he, Max, had saved Sebastian.

Dave didn't seem to care. "So, are you ready for your art lesson?" Dave asked.

"Listen, Dave, I've got news for you," sighed Max. "I'm blind. Remember?"

"Yeah, I remember. But so what? I'll show you how to feel the shapes of

things with your hands," Dave answered. Max could tell that Dave wasn't going to give up.

"But I can't see a thing," Max snapped. "It would be totally dumb for me to take art lessons!"

"No it wouldn't," Dave shot back at Max. "You could just teach your hands to see."

"I've already done that with my ears," said Max. "When you don't have one of your senses, you have to rely on another sense more."

Dave looked confused. "What do you

mean?" he asked.

"Like, I tend to listen very carefully. I really use my ears! I can hear tiny changes in sounds. I can hear all kinds of little scratches and things you may miss," Max explained.

"You mean you can tell the difference between a tape and live music?" asked Dave. He looked doubtful.

Max laughed. "That's the easiest thing in the world! Tapes make lots of noise."

"What kinds of noise?" Dave asked.

"Well, a tape moving over the tape heads makes a hissing noise," Max answered.

"Way cool!" said Dave. "I wish I could hear that."

"I can also hear if there's something wrong with the tape," Max went on.

Suddenly something clicked in Max's mind. He remembered the weird dragging of notes in the music Sebastian had been playing yesterday.

"Dave," Max said slowly. "What have

I done? That was a tape I heard yesterday! Through the wall, I couldn't hear the hissing. But the dragging . . . Sebastian was playing a tape!"

"So, what are you going to do, dude?" asked Dave.

"I have to tell the police," Max sighed.

"Hey, wait a minute," Dave said. "Will they believe you and your ears? Maybe you'll end up getting in trouble if you tell."

Max shook his head. "I don't know," he mumbled.

"Besides," Dave added. "That guy is crazy. If you tell, he might try to hurt you, too!"

"Then I have to go into his apartment and find that tape! If I have the evidence, the police will have to believe me," cried Max. "And Sebastian wouldn't dare hurt me," he added under his breath.

"I'm going with you," said Dave. "For this you need another pair of eyes!"

# **CHAPTER**
# 4

Dave gave Max a hand. "This is creepy," whispered Dave as they climbed through Sebastian's ground-floor window. Max had listened at the apartment wall for a long time. That's how they knew Sebastian had gone out.

"Meow," purred Sebastian's cat Ebony.

"Scat!" hissed Dave at the cat. "Go away!"

"Never mind the cat! Quick! Tell me what you see," Max said to Dave once they were inside.

"Piles of papers," answered Dave. "Wait! There's the tape deck."

"See if there's a tape labeled Mozart

and Bach in there. And hurry!" ordered Max.

"Nothing. It's empty!" groaned Dave.

"Check around. Check the piano. Check the tape case," whispered Max. He was listening hard. What if Sebastian came back while they were still in the apartment?

"Here's something," said Dave.

"Read the label to me," said Max.

"Mozart, Concerto Number 24 in E Minor," read Dave. "Bach Inventions. Weird stuff!"

"That's it!" said Max. "Now let's get out of . . ."

Just then Max heard the sound of a key in the front door. A second later, the door slammed. Max and Dave froze.

"Hide!" ordered Dave.

"Where?" whispered Max.

"Behind the piano," Dave answered. He grabbed Max's arm and dragged him across the room. "It's better than nothing."

Max and Dave crouched down as far as they could. Just then the sound of hurried footsteps entered the room. They held their breath. There was some shuffling of papers. Then the footsteps went into another room.

Max felt something wet touch his hand.

"Meow." Sebastian's cat had followed the boys under the piano.

"Meow." The cat was licking Max's fingers.

"Ebony?" Sebastian called from the other end of the apartment. "Where are you? What's all that yowling?"

Ebony meowed even louder.

Max heard Sebastian's footsteps. The footsteps were getting louder—and closer.

"Oh, no!" whispered Max. "What are we going to do?"

"I've got an idea," Dave whispered back. He pulled a small piece of clay from out of his pocket. He quickly molded it into a small ball. Then Dave rolled the clay ball across the floor. Ebony forgot about the boys and went chasing after the ball.

Sebastian entered the room and stopped short. "There you are," he said. The boys started shaking.

Sebastian picked up Ebony and stroked her fur. He didn't see the clay ball right under his left foot. He didn't see the two boys right under the piano legs.

"Hey, dude, we have to get out of here!" whispered Dave.

"No kidding," Max whispered back. "Somehow we've got to get Sebastian to stay out of this room long enough for us to get back out the window."

"Too bad we can't get someone to ring the doorbell," suggested Dave.

This gave Max an idea. He knocked lightly on the wall next to the piano: two knocks—pause—then three knocks.

"What are you doing?" gasped Dave. "Be quiet!"

"Don't worry," whispered Max. "I just figured out how to make the doorbell ring."

Seconds later, Sebastian's doorbell rang. Dave grabbed Max. As Sebastian opened the door, Dave and Max shot out

from behind the piano. They made it to the window and climbed through.

"Do you still have the tape?" Max asked Dave as they climbed through the open window in Max's apartment.

"You bet!" said Dave. "But what was that knocking bit?"

"That's our danger code. Mom and I worked it out a long time ago," Max explained as he grabbed his cane and headed out of the room. He continued out the front door. Then Max tapped his way across the hall. He asked his mother why she was in the hall. Sebastian sounded annoyed. He slammed his door.

"I thought I heard the danger code from next door," Max's mother said once they were back inside their apartment.

"You did, Mom," said Max. Then he and Dave told her what had happened.

"We'd better call the police," Mrs. Burnett said grimly.

Half an hour later, a squad car was

outside the building. Sebastian was arrested again and put in the car.

Once again all the neighbors were in the hallway. Everyone wanted to know what had happened.

There was a loud meowing. Max felt something brushing against his leg. He bent down to pet Ebony. "Who's going to take care of Ebony, Mom?"

Mrs. Burnett smiled.

"I guess you are, Max. You've made a furry friend there."

The detective walked over to Max and Dave. "That was a dangerous thing you did," the detective said. "Even if you did help us solve the crime. Maybe you'll both end up detectives, but wait until you're old enough to apply for the job! Still, you make a good team."

"I know," said Max. "Dave's my eyes!"

"And Max here is my ears!" said Dave.